19

DATE DUE

			PRINTED IN U.S.A.

FINDING a CAREER

Careers If You Like Science

Gail Snyder

ReferencePoint Press®

San Diego, CA

About the Author
Gail Snyder is a freelance writer and advertising copywriter who has written twenty-five books for young readers. She has a degree in journalism from Pennsylvania State University and lives in Chalfont, Pennsylvania, with her husband, Hal Marcovitz.

Picture Credits
Cover: Depositphotos/dmbaker
17: Depositphotos/osmar01
35: Depositphotos/Kalinovsky
69: Depositphotos/toxawww

© 2017 ReferencePoint Press, Inc.
Printed in the United States

For more information, contact:
ReferencePoint Press, Inc.
PO Box 27779
San Diego, CA 92198
www.ReferencePointPress.com

LIBRARY OF CONGRESS CATALOGING-IN-PUBLICATION DATA

Names: Snyder, Gail, author.
Title: Careers if you like science / by Gail Snyder.
Description: San Diego, CA : ReferencePoint Press, Inc., [2016] | Audience: Grades 9 to 12. | Includes bibliographical references and index.
Identifiers: LCCN 2016023548 (print) | LCCN 2016024550 (ebook) | ISBN 9781682820063 (hardback) | ISBN 9781682820070 (eBook)
Subjects: LCSH: Science--Vocational guidance--Juvenile literature. | Vocational guidance.
Classification: LCC Q147 .S65 2016 (print) | LCC Q147 (ebook) | DDC 502.3--dc23
LC record available at https://lccn.loc.gov/2016023548

CONTENTS

Introduction: Scientists Rule

If you like science you might want to research the following hypotheses: Since you are curious and eager to learn how the physical world around you operates, could one of many hundreds of possible careers in science lead you to a career that pays well and is very much in demand from a wide variety of employers? Also, could a career in science enable you to make discoveries that would satisfy your desire to contribute to society? As you research these questions, you will find there is abundant evidence that studying science—particularly for students who also enjoy math, engineering, and technology—will have verifiable rewards.

The website CareerCast.com lists such science-related jobs as biomedical engineer, geologist, medical laboratory technician, pharmacist, physicist, environmental engineer, and veterinarian among the top fifty careers for salaries as well as the potential for advancement. Moreover, according to a 2014 report by the Pew Research Center, a Washington, DC–based group that studies a variety of social issues, 78 percent of people who majored in science and engineering in college reported that they are now working in jobs related to their majors. By comparison, just 59 percent of social science, liberal arts, and education majors said they are employed in jobs related to their degrees.

Skills Sought by Employers

With the high price of college tuition it makes sense to choose an education in line with what employers are seeking. Therefore, if students must take out loans to finance their college educations, they would find it easier to repay their loans if they earn higher salaries after completing their degrees. Earning a college degree in science could help do that for you. Whether science majors concentrate on biological, physical, or earth sciences they will still come away with traits many employers value. These include well-honed problem-solving skills that employ creativity and persistence to surmount failure; the ability to gather data, analyze it, and reach conclusions both independently and in teams; and being able to clearly convey their findings in written reports and oral presentations. These are the same skills the National Association of Colleges and Employers (NACE) has identified as most sought after by employers in a 2015 survey. The NACE is a nonprofit organization that shares information connecting employers with college placement services.

There is no shortage of places to put these skills to work. Scientists might work for colleges and universities where they may teach and do research, especially if they have graduate degrees. These degrees include a master's degree and a doctorate degree, also known as a PhD. Typically, a master's degree takes another two years or more of college to attain after the student has earned an undergraduate degree, also known as a bachelor's degree. Students who want to go on to earn a PhD can expect to spend at least another two years after their master's degree is completed—and very often, three years or more—before they are awarded their doctorate degrees.

After completing their education, there is a wide array of opportunities awaiting graduates with degrees in the sciences. One employer anxious to hire graduates with degrees in the sciences is the federal government, which employs scientists to work in food and drug safety, environmental protection, space exploration, weapons development, and eradication of diseases. Private employers with a need for scientists include pharmaceutical companies, aerospace companies, and energy companies. Some graduates with degrees in science find jobs as science teachers in public schools, private schools, and universities. Physicians as well as others with degrees in medical-related fields may work in hospitals and physicians' offices contributing to the welfare of patients.

Working in Offices, Clinics, and Crime Scenes

It is also possible to establish a career as a professional who writes about science rather than actually practicing it. For example, science writer Tina Saey translates scientific concepts into language nonscientists can understand. These articles are typically published in general interest magazines and websites. In an article in the *Science Teacher*, the journal of the National Science Teachers Association, Saey says,

> Being a science writer is fun, rewarding and challenging. I have watched surgeries, held a preserved human brain, visited laboratories, and gone out in the field with scientists. . . . I took a trip to Boston to visit a sleep study clinic. Researchers were studying people's natural rhythms and investigating what variables—green or very bright lights—most effectively reset their biological clocks.

The long-standing notion that all scientists wear white lab coats, look through microscopes, or work in sterile laboratories is not necessarily true. Environmental engineers, who work in the field of environmental science, might just as well wear hard hats and spend time in the field, heading operations to clean up hazardous materials spills and other environmental dangers. Other scientists may wear latex gloves and protective booties to gather crime scene evidence as forensic science technologists. Or as veterinarians, they may go into a stable in blue jeans and boots to treat an ill horse. Scientists might also find themselves wearing business suits, spending most of their time in front of computer screens in corporate offices.

No matter where they work or which fields of science they may choose, people who study science will come away with skill sets that make them highly valuable to employers and help them understand the natural world better. Backgrounds in science also assist people in making discoveries that can improve the lives of humans and animals. The journey toward a career in science also enables students to discover their talents and interests, helping them learn more about themselves.

Biomedical Engineer

What Biomedical Engineers Do

Biomedical engineers are not typical scientists. As with other scientists, they study biology, chemistry, and mathematics, and they learn about scientific method, techniques of experimentation, and how to interpret results. But unlike a lot of other scientists they spend a lot of time with machines—figuring out how they work and making them work better.

Biomedical engineers design devices that solve human health problems. They contribute to cutting-edge technology that helps revolutionize health care. Among the projects under development are tiny needles that can be used to administer drugs to specific places in the body. This is thought to be a much more effective drug delivery system than giving patients drugs in pill form. Some biomedical engineers work with human cells, nurturing them to create artificial organs. Biomedical engineers also design and develop new prosthetic limbs that are much more nimble than the cumbersome limbs patients have used for decades. For example, a new prosthetic hand under development is so nimble that it is capable of picking up a single cracker without causing it to crumble.

The website CNNMoney.com has placed biomedical engineer at the top of its list of best jobs in America. According to the article, "It's a career that gives back to society by helping to improve world health. It's also highly flexible, with positions in universities, labs, industry and regulatory agencies."

Who Hires Biomedical Engineers?

With a degree in biomedical engineering you could find yourself working in a variety of settings. According to the Bureau of Labor Statistics (BLS), biomedical engineers find jobs with companies that design and manufacture medical equipment and supplies, create electronic instrumentation used to diagnose and monitor illnesses, and design drug delivery systems. Biomedical engineers may also work for the US Food and Drug Administration (FDA), which must approve all medical devices before they are made available to patients. At the FDA, biomedical engineers inspect and test new devices to ensure they meet safety requirements and perform as well as their manufacturers claim. Once these devices pass FDA scrutiny, biomedical engineers can still play a role in the process of bringing these devices to market. Some work for

A Rewarding Feeling

"My favorite thing about engineering is seeing something transition from an idea on paper into an actual piece of hardware. It's amazing to see what all your hard work, planning and designing (and then redesigning ten more times) can result in. It isn't easy, but it is the most rewarding and proud feeling to see your finished product operating how it was supposed to."

Michaelina Dupnik, quoted in ECN Magazine, "How This Biomedical Engineer Landed Her Dream Job," January 9, 2015. www.ecnmag.com.

law firms that specialize in writing patents for the devices, which ensure that manufacturers are guaranteed profits through making and selling the instruments.

In fact, what biomedical engineers do varies so much that there are no tasks typically associated with them. That means that as a biomedical engineer you might find yourself working with medical personnel who need to know how to use the equipment you designed, making certain biomedical equipment is safe and effective, writing research papers that present your findings to colleagues, designing software for running high-tech medical equipment, or supervising the work of less experienced colleagues.

Many Specialties

Injury biomechanics, which is the study of how living things move, is one of the many specialties of biomedical engineering. Cynthia Bir is a biomedical engineer who specializes in injury biomechanics. In an interview on the *Working Mother* magazine website she describes a typical workday at her job in the Center for Trauma, Violence & Injury Prevention at the University of Southern California's Keck School of Medicine. She says:

> I basically research all the ways the body becomes injured and how we might prevent those injuries. Every day is different. One day I might be writing a grant and the next day I might be analyzing data from a project. I study everything from body armor to football helmets to ways to prevent injuries. I conduct studies both in the field and in the lab, looking at the mechanics of injuries and the ways we can prevent them.

Bir works forty to sixty hours a week, often taking work home with her.

Biomedical engineers can also specialize. Some work with biomaterials while others work with artificial devices that are incorporated into the body's natural systems, such as artificial heart valves, dental implants, and hip replacements. Among the other specialties are bioinstrumentation, in which engineers develop devices used in the diagnosis and treatment of disease, and clinical engineering, which focuses on developing databases for medical instruments and patient records used by hospitals. Medical imaging is another specialty of biomedical engineering. Engineers who focus on this area develop better ways for physicians to see into the human body. Also, some biomedical engineers specialize in systems physiology, in which engineers study how the human body works to help them gain an insight into why organs and other parts of the body may fail.

Another specialty is rehabilitative engineering, in which biomedical engineers work with disabled people to restore some of their lost functions through assistive devices. Over the years, patients have been aided by such devices as wheelchairs, scooters, and prosthetic limbs. In recent years, biomedical engineers have focused on designing such devices as kitchen implements with cushioned grips, helping people with severe arthritis manipulate can openers, spatulas, and other common kitchen tools. Says Gary Downey, a Kansas City, Missouri–based rehabilitation engineer:

> Between ourselves and every task we do lies some sort of interface that helps us accomplish that task. This interface takes many different forms. . . . A few interface examples might be a computer mouse, a doorknob, a telephone, a screwdriver, a light switch, or a blender. Most of us don't give much thought to using these interfaces. We just use them. For someone with a disability, however, these interfaces can present a huge barrier to the task they wish to accomplish.

Downey was interviewed by a website maintained by the Rehabilitation Engineering and Assistive Technology Society of North America (RESNA) chapter at Stanford University in California.

Among the devices that Downey says have recently been designed for impaired people are a camera mount for a wheelchair used by a photographer who is unable to walk; a microscope that can be focused with a lever, rather than a knob, intended for laboratory workers with limited ability to use their hands; and a vacuum cleaner mount for a wheelchair for a custodian who cannot walk. He says, "For most of us technology makes things easier. For people with a disability, technology makes things possible."

Who Makes a Good Biomedical Engineer?

If you are thinking about a career as a biomedical engineer you'll want to consider whether you possess the most common characteristics of people already working in the field. Biomedical engineers are interested in how the human body works because they have a desire to help people overcome illnesses and disabilities. They are fascinated with how machines and electronic devices work because mechanical and electronic apparatuses are often used to make daily life easier for people in those situations. "Many of the answers to medical problems are often similar to answers to engineering problems. I love that you can utilize tools and expertise that's been developed over the last 100-plus years in mechanical engineering to solve problems related to human health," says Jonathan Vande Geest, an assistant professor of biomedical engineering at the University of Arizona. Vande Geest was interviewed by a website maintained by his school's College of Engineering.

Many biomedical engineers must be comfortable with making speeches or leading forums in front of audiences. Biomedical engineers who apply for grants often have to make public presentations to government agencies and private foundations that fund research—sometimes awarding the engineers millions of dollars to pursue their projects.

Education and Training

A bachelor of science (BS) degree is necessary to begin a career as a biomedical engineer, but there are two options worth exploring for getting such a degree. Some students enroll in a university

No Day Is the Same

"One of the best parts of my job is that every day is different, so I don't have a typical day. I could easily be helping one of my students in my chemistry lab to prepare a clinical sample in the morning, join another student at the MRI [magnetic resonance imaging] scanner to acquire medical images around lunch hour, meet with a student on campus to discuss graphs and figures for a manuscript, and meet with yet another student on campus in the late afternoon or early evening to analyze data using a computer program."

Mark Pagel, quoted in Colleges & Degrees, "Interview with Biomedical Engineering Professor Mark 'Marty' Pagel." www.collegesanddegrees.com.

that has an accredited program in biomedical engineering. Other students study another form of engineering such as electrical engineering, and take life science courses as electives. Both paths are equally acceptable.

Students can also choose electives that could lead to an area of specialization, and take advantage of co-op or internship opportunities. A co-op—short for cooperative—is a program sponsored by a government agency or private corporation offering promising students opportunities to obtain on-the-job training in their fields of study. Typically, co-op students take one or more semesters off from their university studies to work full-time for employers. Internships also provide on-the-job training; they may also be provided on a full-time basis but many internships are part time and served during semesters.

For many biomedical engineers the BS degree is only the beginning of their educations. As many as two-thirds of biomedical engineers seek advanced degrees, according to Indiana University's School of Engineering and Technology, one of 132 American universities that offer graduate degrees in biomedical engineering, according to the website findengineeringschools.org. Graduates who want to continue their educations in biomedical engineering often pursue master's degrees and doctorate degrees.

Future Outlook

The job outlook for biomedical engineers is well above average, driven in part by the increasing health needs of aging members of the population who hope to take advantage of the latest medical devices and technology to prolong and optimize their lives. Such engineers earned average salaries of $86,950 in 2014. The highest salaries, according to the BLS, were earned by individuals working in research and development, who made an average of $97,160, while the lowest salaries were found among employees who worked for hospitals. Their wages averaged $72,060. While experiencing a healthy 23 percent growth rate, the number of new biomedical engineering jobs is expected to grow by only a little more than five thousand jobs between now and 2024 because the field is still relatively small.

Says W. Mark Saltzman, a professor of biomedical engineering at Yale University in Connecticut and author of the book *Biomedical Engineering: Bridging Medicine and Technology*:

> We know that modern medicine is built on steady progress in science, but is just as heavily dependent on innovations in engineering. Engineers are the ones who transfer scientific knowledge into useful products, devices and methods; therefore, progress in biomedical engineering is arguably more central to our experience of modern medicine than advances in science.

Find Out More

American Institute for Medical and Biological Engineering
1400 I St. NW, Suite 235
Washington, DC 20005
phone: (202) 496-9660
website: http://aimbe.org

The nonprofit group represents the interests of some fifty thousand medical and biological engineering professionals before lawmakers and government agencies. By accessing the Educate link on the group's website, students can learn about the profession and what they need to do to prepare for careers as biological and medical engineers.

Biomedical Engineering Society
8201 Corporate Dr.
Landover, MD 20785
phone: (301) 459-1999
website: www.bmes.org

The society is the world's leading professional organization for biomedical engineering. Activities include communicating recent advances, discoveries, and inventions and promoting education and professional development.

IEEE Engineering in Medicine & Biology Society
445 Hoes Ln.
Piscataway, NJ 08854
phone: (732) 981-3433
website: www.embs.org

The society is part of the Institute of Electrical and Electronics Engineers (IEEE). The society promotes biomedical engineering and offers conferences and other professional development activities for its members. By accessing the Member Communities link on the group's website, students can find information on pursuing careers in biomedical engineering.

Institute of Biological Engineering
446 E. High St., Suite 10
Lexington, KY 40507
phone: (859) 977-7450
website: www.ibe.org

The Institute of Biological Engineering offers scholarships; sets professional standards; fosters cooperation between academics, industry, and government; and promotes public understanding of biological engineering products. It offers meetings, conferences, and publications.

Environmental Scientist

Protecting the Earth's Resources

There are few areas of employment that can potentially have a bigger impact on the world than those that center on environmental science. This is particularly true today when threats to human health and the planet's survival seem so imminent. A major concern focuses on global warming, also known as climate change, which scientists believe could have disastrous consequences for life on earth. Yet these challenges also offer opportunities for students who train as environmental scientists for careers that could put them at the forefront of shaping environmental policy. Among these careers are climate change analyst, whose job revolves around predicting the environmental consequences of global warming; environmental geologist, who prevents contamination of the soil and searches for underground resources such as water; and environmental engineer, who finds ways to protect the public health by reducing pollution.

This area of science may appeal to anyone who is distressed by the dire warnings about the future of the planet, who enjoys using research skills, who likes to solve big problems, and who has the curiosity to explore many different areas of study. These areas include geology, meteorology, ecology, biology, physics, oceanography, and chemistry.

Even better, those who pursue careers in the environmental sciences are likely to find satisfying and well-paying careers in fields where the jobs are sure to grow. They would find those jobs at organizations or foundations dedicated to protecting the environment. Also, environmental scientists can find jobs at universities where they might work in classrooms or laboratories. Many environmental scientists are hired by industries or governments to help clean up properties where the soil or groundwater is polluted.

Someone who pursues a career in environmental science would be at the vanguard of a movement whose goal is nothing less than sustaining life on the planet. Daniel D. Chiras, who teaches environmental policy at the University of Denver, in his book *Environmental Science*, writes,

> Over time, many of us have discovered that we've been addressing environmental problems a bit superficially. We've learned that most efforts are nothing more than stopgap measures—solutions that treat the symptoms while neglecting the underlying root causes. Environmental scientists and others now recognize that to create lasting solutions we must address their root causes.

What Climate Change Analysts Do

Since the 1980s, most scientists have been in agreement that earth's climate is warming due to carbon emissions in the atmosphere and that the biggest cause of this is the burning of fossil fuels—oil, natural gas, and coal. Scientists have predicted dramatic consequences due to climate change: destruction of species and habitats; rising ocean levels, which could flood coastal cities; and an increase in destructive storms.

Climate change analysts use mathematical models to draw

To check water quality, an environmental scientist tests for chemicals and other pollutants. Some environmental scientists help governments and industries analyze and clean up polluted soil or groundwater.

conclusions from copious amounts of climate data. The data might relate to ocean temperatures, carbon emissions, and the melting of the world's ice sheets. Ordinarily, this type of data is gathered by other people; climate change analysts do not usually go into the field to collect their own data. Rather, they interpret data to explain how changing climate conditions affect the economy, food supply, and plant and animal populations.

Climate change analysts interact with legislators, regulatory agencies, corporations, environmental organizations, and the general public through speeches, policy papers, and recommendations on what ought to be done to limit the damage caused by rising temperatures. Their work in determining what is likely to happen in the future if current trends continue is used by legislators and other government officials so they can make more informed decisions on environmental matters. For example, climate change analysts might testify on the impacts of how using energy-efficient vehicles would improve the environment. Or, they might study the impacts of drilling for oil in the Arctic National Wildlife Refuge, or how climate change could affect food production in the future. Successful climate change analysts are detail oriented, analytical, capable of translating complicated scientific concepts into layperson's language, and passionate about putting the practical aspects of science to good use through policies and education.

As a climate change analyst for the London, England–based Institute for Public Policy Research, Jenny Bird helped write a report for the British government showing how it is possible for Great Britain to reduce its fossil fuel use by 80 percent by 2050. In an interview with the website of *New Scientist*, she said, "Right from the start I had freedom to pursue my own research and ideas for policies that will improve lives and contribute to the climate change debate. It's very liberating."

Geologists: Studying the Past Makes a Great Future

As a geologist, you would learn about history on its grandest scale—the earth's history. In performing your duties you would bring to bear lessons from the planet's past on the problems people face in the future. If you like being outside and getting your hands dirty, you may be excited about opportunities to study fossils, minerals, ancient and active volcanos, earthquakes, and soil and beach erosion.

Sharing Facts About Climate Change

"A long time ago I was working in the energy field, and it became clear to me the biggest issue surrounding energy and the way we use energy is climate change. Twenty-five or more years ago I got the sense this was going to be the issue of our time, and that I had a responsibility because I knew something about it and I could help communicate about it. I have no illusions that I'm going to solve this problem single-handedly. I see myself as a link in the chain. I just feel like I want to do the most important thing that I can do to help, so that's what I'm doing. It drives me."

Susan Hassol, quoted in NASA, "Communicating Climate Change," Center for Climate Sciences, May 2011. http://climatesciences.jpl.nasa.gov.

Many different types of employers seek professionals who study the earth. Geologists can expect to find jobs at science museums as well as local, state, and federal agencies. Also, energy companies—those that seek new sources of oil, natural gas, and coal—hire geologists to find new deposits.

There are about twenty areas of specialization within the field of geology. Among them is environmental geology. Environmental geologists decide where to locate huge industrial projects, such as nuclear power plants or landfills that span hundreds of acres.

Geologist Sandie Will heads a department of the Florida state government that searches for new sources of groundwater. These sources are known as aquifers. They are located hundreds of feet below the surface and can be accessed only by drilling wells. In an essay published on the website Rock-Head Sciences, Will described some of what her job entails:

It's very interesting to get behind the rig with the drillers to see the cores come out of the ground and all the fossils and the characteristics of the different rock types. I also like to see when the geologists graph all the data together . . . to determine the depths where formation changes. . . . Other interesting field work includes seeing the water level changes through time plotted on graphs as the aquifer responds to pump tests to see how deep the drawdown will be, how quickly the water level will [stabilize] while pumping, and how long water levels will take to return to normal once pumping is stopped. All of this will give us an idea of how well aquifers will produce water if needed for future water supplies.

Environmental Engineers: Protecting the Air, Soil, and Water

Environmental engineers help design projects that preserve the environment, such as sewage treatment plants that clean wastewater before returning it to streams or designing landfills so that hazardous materials do not leak into the environment. They also use their expertise to help clean up the environment. For example, an environmental engineer may be called in to devise ways to remove soil that has been contaminated by a chemical leak at a nearby factory.

In 2012, environmental engineers from the Massachusetts Institute of Technology (MIT) devised a new way to clean up oil that is spilled into large bodies of water. Their research was prompted by the 2010 explosion on the *Deepwater Horizon* oil drilling rig in the Gulf of Mexico. The explosion caused a gusher of oil to open below the rig, causing a spill of more than 200 million gallons of oil into the gulf. The spill caused widespread environmental damage to ocean life and took months to clean up, mostly using low-tech methods such as laying miles of oil containment booms—which are essentially long floating tubes—to encircle and trap the oil so it could be suctioned out of the gulf.

The MIT scheme involves submerging cylinder-shaped magnets into the path of the oil. Since oil contains concentrations of metallic substances, the magnets would trap the oil inside the cylinders.

Commenting on the MIT method, chemical engineer Ronald Rosensweig, an expert on oil spill containment, told the website MITNews, "This oil-spill problem has not really been worked on intensively that I know of, and of course it's a big problem. . . . In a lot of cases, [oil and water] are pretty much equal in density: Some of the oil sinks, some of it floats, and a lot of it is in between. The magnetic hook could, hopefully, make separation faster and better."

Educational Requirements

Careers in environmental sciences require college educations with at least a bachelor of science degree. The degree may be in environmental science or perhaps mathematics, geology, earth science, environmental policy, ecology, environmental engineering, chemistry, physics, or engineering. Anyone who would like to have a career teaching at the university level would need a PhD.

The subjects studied vary according to the direction a student takes. Climate change analysts, for instance, study mathematics, physics, computer science, economics, and public policy as undergraduates. In order to be able to do sophisticated computer modeling a master's degree or doctorate is necessary. Geology majors learn mathematics, social science, environmental science, and concepts relating to streams, flooding, and climate change. Time in the classroom is augmented by laboratory work, hands-on study in nature, and, ideally, working as an intern with a government agency or private company that employs geologists. Students seeking environmental engineering degrees would be expected to take a wide variety of science courses, particularly chemistry and biology. In addition, while in college students would be expected to study water supplies, waste management, and management of natural resources.

High Salaries, Growing Demand

Not only do environmental science careers play a role in making the planet a healthier place but they also offer high salaries. The

Geologists Seek Adventure

"The geology field is very interesting and rewarding, but be prepared to work long, hard days in conditions that can be challenging including thunderstorms and rain, extreme heat and cold, remote areas, downtown cities with high traffic, as well as with numerous critters including snakes, spiders, ants, etc. of all different varieties. In addition, you could spend numerous days traveling throughout the month. If you're adventurous, though, this job will be right up your alley! Depending on the industry, you could end up seeing numerous states and countries, as well as all different types of geologic settings."

Sandie Will, "What's a Typical Day Like as a Geologist?," Rock-Head Sciences, May 2, 2014. http://rockheadsciences.com.

average 2012 salary for climate change analysts was $66,250, while geologists were earning an average of $91,920. As of 2014, environmental engineers were enjoying average salaries of $84,560.

In addition to good pay, the environmental science field is experiencing healthy job growth. According to the Bureau of Labor Statistics, environmental science positions are growing at 11 percent per year. Climate change analyst positions are expected to grow between 14 percent and 20 percent from now until 2022. Also growing by as much as 21 percent are jobs for geologists, a profession expected to add 17,300 new positions by 2022. Meanwhile 6,800 environmental engineering positions are expected to be added to the workforce. This represents 12 percent growth in the field through 2024, when there are expected to be more than 55,000 jobs for environmental engineers.

There will always be new environmental concerns to tackle and a need for better solutions for doing business and informing legislators and the public about policies that can make more efficient use of the natural resources available to people. Those who study environmental science can be on the forefront of developing and sharing that cutting-edge information as they engage in work that makes a difference in the quality of life on earth.

Find Out More

American Academy of Environmental Engineers and Scientists
147 Old Solomons Island Rd., Suite 303
Annapolis, MD 21401
phone: (410) 266-3311
fax: (410) 266-7653
website: www.aaees.org
e-mail: info@aaees.org

The professional association representing environmental engineers establishes procedures that guide the profession, including a certification program for members. The academy also publishes papers on important environmental issues and sponsors a program to mentor students pursuing careers as environmental engineers.

Association for Environmental Studies and Sciences (AESS)
1101 Seventeenth St. NW, No. 250
Washington, DC 20036
phone: (202) 530-5810
website: https://aessonline.org

Members of the AESS include more than one thousand students and academics representing environmental programs around the world. By joining AESS, members can access an online database of job opportunities in environmental science.

Association of Climate Change Officers
PO Box 53249
Washington, DC 20009
phone: (202) 496-7390
website: www.accoonline.org

The Association of Climate Change Officers is an educational association for people who work for climate change in 150 organizations in industry, government, nonprofits, and universities. Its members engage in networking, research sharing, education, and training.

Geological Society of America
PO Box 9140
Boulder, CO 80301
phone: (303) 357-1000
website: www.geosociety.org

More than one hundred years old, the Geological Society of America is committed to the professional development of its twenty-six thousand members in 115 countries. The society is the foremost association for geologists and offers publications, networking opportunities, and career resources.

National Association of Environmental Professionals
PO Box 460
Collingswood, NJ 07108
website: www.naep.org

The National Association of Environmental Professionals offers conferences, scholarships, publications, and more to fulfill its mission of enhancing ethical and proficient decision making for environmental professionals. There are student chapters for people studying environmental science.

Student Conservation Association
689 River Rd.
Charlestown, NH 03603
phone: (603) 543-1700
website: www.thesca.org

Members of the Student Conservation Association, who must be at least fifteen years old, learn about sustainability and conservation and provide hands-on service by protecting and restoring national parks, marine sanctuaries, and community spaces. With chapters in every state, the organization has worked with seventy-five thousand students since it was established in 1957.

Forensic Science Technician

Making Crime Pay

You may be familiar with the work of a forensic science technician—also known as a crime scene investigator—through one of the *CSI* TV shows or the novels authored by Arthur Conan Doyle featuring detective Sherlock Holmes. Readers of Doyle's books know Holmes was as likely to use a microscope to search for evidence as he was to track down an eyewitness. Fans of *CSI* can see dramatizations of forensic science technicians gathering evidence and subjecting it to scientific analyses as they build cases against suspects in crimes. In real life, as in Doyle's stories and on *CSI*, forensic science technicians study the evidence in a laboratory, analyze the evidence, draw conclusions, and testify about their findings in court. "People all over the world are fascinated by crime, its investigations and its solutions," write Jay Siegel and Kathy Mirakovits, in their book *Forensic Science: The Basics*. "People enjoy using clues to solve puzzles and problems. They are concerned with violent crime and want to do something about it. All of these factors feed into the popularity

Communicating Their Findings

"A lot of our work ends up in a report, or in conversation, with an attorney, and these are the decision makers—the people that need to know the reliability, or unreliability, of our findings. Defendants might take a plea bargain, or prosecutors might offer one. It's about getting information from the brains of the analysts to the brains of those making the decision—the judge, jury or litigators—so they can try to make the best possible decision about a case, whatever that might be, especially if the case has the potential to be resolved before it goes to trial."

Keith Inman, quoted in *Forensic Magazine*, "The Future of Crime Scene Forensic Science: An Interview with Keith Inman," February 10, 2015. www.forensicmag.com.

of forensic science." Siegel is a professor of forensic science at Indiana University while Mirakovits teaches forensic science at Portage Northern High School in Portage, Michigan.

For those who can tolerate a high "ick" factor, working in forensics can be satisfying. Forensic science technicians must be prepared to sink their gloved hands into blood and other bodily fluids, and remain steely enough to take an analytical view of the effects of bullets, knives, and other lethal objects.

How Do You Become a Forensic Science Technician?

If you want to put your love of science to work as a forensic science technician you may need to begin your career by enrolling in a police academy. Many forensic science technicians have first trained as police officers. After graduating from the academy and joining local police departments, they transfer into the forensic science departments when opportunities arise.

The route to a career in forensic science does not necessarily have to go through a police academy. Many forensic science technicians find jobs in their profession by first attaining a bachelor's degree in chemistry, biology, or forensic science (some thirty universities offer forensic science as a major.) As with other scientific fields, some students go on to obtain graduate degrees in forensic science. A master's degree enables them to specialize in particular fields. Possibilities include ballistics (the science of how bullets and other projectiles are fired) as well as fingerprinting. Some master's degree programs train forensic scientists in the analysis of DNA—the unique chemical thumbprint found in blood and other bodily fluids and tissue that helps identify victims and perpetrators. Other students focus on the analysis of handwriting, which can also be a valuable tool used to identify suspects.

Qualities of a Forensic Science Technician

A love of science is one ingredient that goes into the making of a forensic science technician. Forensic science technicians also possess calm demeanors and the ability to work well with other professionals such as lawyers and detectives as well as doctors who may be called in to examine wounds sustained by victims.

Also, the forensic science technician handles evidence that could be used to convict somebody of a crime—and send that person to jail. Therefore, the technician must have the discipline to adhere to strict protocols and guidelines. Breaking the rules might taint the evidence, which means it cannot be used in court. Excellent verbal and written communication skills are helpful as well. In his book *A Survey of the Forensic Sciences*, Randall R. Skelton, a professor of forensic science at the University of Montana, writes,

Find out all you can about the forensic science you are interested in, and be realistic about yourself in deciding whether you are really cut out for it or not. . . . If you are the type of person who craves excitement, do you really want to be a trace evidence examiner and spend your days counting dust grains and examining hairs through a microscope? Can you be meticulous about keeping good records? Can you be depended on to do your analyses thoroughly? Can you work well as a member of a team? Can you work well independently? Can you face the prospect of testifying regularly in court? Are you willing to drop what you are doing to go process a crime scene at a moment's notice?

Where and When Do They Work?

Graduates seeking careers as forensic science technicians will find most jobs available in law enforcement agencies on the local, state, and federal levels. Among these employers are local and state police departments as well as federal agencies such as the FBI. Also, local medical examiners—also known as forensic pathologists—may send forensic science technicians into the field to gather evidence. The office of the medical examiner is typically maintained by local or state governments. In addition, the branches of the military also maintain their own police forces and utilize forensic science technicians to assist in their investigations in cases that involve military personnel. Some jobs are available

What No One Prepares You For

"I wasn't really prepared for a couple of things. One of them is the pressure of the job. Most laboratories are going to be chronically understaffed and overworked because they are by and large parts of police departments. You're down at the bottom of this funding ladder, and it's very difficult to get the financial and manpower support that you need to do a really good job. There are also some subtle pressures. Scientists are trained to be objective—you get into the field and there are these subtle pressures that come from the district attorney or the investigator. That kind of pressure can become unnerving."

Ronald L. Singer, quoted in CriminalJusticePrograms.com, "Q&A with Criminalist, Ronald L. Singer, M.S." www.criminaljusticeprograms.com.

in the private sector—these jobs are typically found in private law firms pursuing lawsuits alleging that deaths were caused by negligent acts committed by others. These law firms employ forensic science technicians to gather and analyze evidence.

Because crimes happen at all hours, forensic science technicians may be called in to work unexpectedly at any hour, day or night. On the job, they may be called on to work in inhospitable conditions, in all types of weather. If, for example, a body is found in a swamp and discovered during a downpour, the forensic science technician assigned to the case would be called on to traipse into the mud and endure the elements while performing proper evidence-gathering techniques. However, much of their work is also pursued indoors in the crime lab where evidence is analyzed.

Typical Day

Crime scene investigation may look pretty straightforward, at least where television programming is concerned. But the reality is different. On TV, forensic science technicians seem to instantly determine what happens at a crime scene, easily pinpointing the exact time and cause of death. "They never have to go to the literature, as we do," says Patricia McFeely, a forensic pathologist at the University of New Mexico Health Sciences Center, who was interviewed by NBC News.

Max Houck directs the Forensic Science Initiative at West Virginia University. In an interview with NBC News he said that, unlike on *CSI*, where the characters drive Hummers and dress stylishly, real forensic science technicians generally do neither. He said, "As I tell my students, it's less about wearing leather pants and driving Hummers than it is about wearing a [protective] Tyvek jumpsuit and crawling under somebody's porch and looking for body parts."

Moreover, forensic science technicians who move into supervisory roles may find themselves seeing to all manner of administrative tasks before they are able to don their rubber gloves and perform the tasks they have been trained to tackle. Jason

Birchfield, a forensic science supervisor for Baltimore County, Maryland, described his typical day in an interview with *NSTA WebNews Digest*:

> I arrive at work early, check with the prior shift to see if any crime scene calls are holding, and determine what additional calls I will be responsible for during the day. I then delegate duties and decide which employees will handle which areas within Baltimore County. As the supervisor, I am required to personally respond to any homicides, suspicious deaths, or police shootings, respond to and process crime scene calls when my shift is short-handed or exceptionally busy, and read and approve the reports and evidence packaging that occurs during my shift.

Cool Tools

Understanding and using technology is a big part of a forensic science technician's job. As that technology changes, each practitioner will need to adapt. One machine they might work with is a spectrometer, which, for example, helps technicians match tiny pieces of glass found on clothing with glass found at a crime scene. Another machine a forensic science technician might use is the video spectral comparator. This machine helps investigators see writing that is not visible with the naked eye. Usually this involves an imprint left by a pen used on a sheet of paper that was torn off a pad. Forensic science technicians may lift fingerprints from the crime scene—one of the newer technologies used is a magnetic fingerprinting dust. In years past, forensic science technicians have applied nonmagnetic dust to the imprint, which would have to be brushed on—a process that could mar the print. Magnetic dust can be lifted off the surface by using a magnet, enabling the technician to save the fingerprint with a reduced chance of marring the impression.

Back at the crime lab, the technician enters the fingerprint into the Integrated Automated Fingerprint Identification System (AFIS), a database that records fingerprints from millions of people who have been arrested. To enter the fingerprints in the database the technician photographs them using a digital camera, then uploads the images into the system where they can be compared with other fingerprints on file.

In explaining the role that technology plays in forensic investigations, Ronald L. Singer, technical and administrative director of the Tarrant County Medical Examiner's Office in Fort Worth, Texas, says,

> We're doing things now with DNA analysis that were simply not possible before. In addition, [Integrated] Automated Fingerprint Identification System—what it will do for you in an hour used to take days or even weeks. We've got databases now not only in fingerprints, but in DNA, in firearms and in shoeprints. One area that has been most impacted is DNA. Now you can actually get a full DNA profile off of the cells that are left behind on the collar of a shirt. You are going to be able to do more and more with less and less.

Singer was interviewed by CriminalJusticePrograms.com, a website that focuses on criminal justice careers.

Future Prospects

Forensic science technicians can expect to make about $55,660 a year in a profession that is expected to grow by 27 percent by 2024. According to the Bureau of Labor Statistics, about 14,400 people were employed as forensic science technicians in 2014; the profession is expected to grow by thirty-nine hundred jobs through 2024. Salaries are higher for forensic science technicians with master's degrees and areas of specialization that set them apart from others. In addition, larger cities with police departments can be expected to pay better than smaller city police departments.

It may be easy to see why television shows and novels about forensic science technicians are so popular. Many people enjoy watching how these professionals use science to solve mysteries, pursue justice, and catch criminals using the often unseen evidence they have left behind.

Find Out More

American Academy of Forensic Sciences
410 N. Twenty-First St.
Colorado Springs, CO 80904
phone: (719) 636-1100
website: www.aafs.org

The American Academy of Forensic Sciences promotes education, research, and collaboration among members of the forensic sciences community. Its Young Forensic Scientists Forum allows recent graduates to acclimate themselves to the profession through their own newsletter and conferences.

Association of Firearm and Tool Mark Examiners
5350 Second St. NW
Albuquerque, NM 87101
phone: (505) 823-4260
website: https://afte.org

The Association of Firearm and Tool Mark Examiners is the international professional organization for people who must accurately identify which tools or guns were used to commit crimes. It produces a quarterly journal and hosts annual six-day training seminars around the country.

Federal Bureau of Investigation (FBI) Laboratory Services
935 Pennsylvania Ave. NW
Washington, DC 20535
phone: (202) 324-3000
website: www.fbi.gov/hq/lab/labhome.htm

The FBI Laboratory Services employs some five hundred scientific experts and special agents. They perform such tasks as examining DNA to help determine guilt or innocence, analyzing fingerprints left at a crime scene, or linking exploded bomb fragments to terrorists.

Forensic Sciences Foundation

410 N. Twenty-First St.
Colorado Springs, CO 80904
phone: (719) 636-1100
website: http://fsf.aafs.org

The Forensic Sciences Foundation's activities include sponsoring seminars and courses for physicians, publishing books on forensic science, giving an award for young forensic scientists, and awarding grants for forensic research. Visitors to the foundation's website can find information on scholarships awarded to students pursuing degrees in forensic science.

International Association for Identification

2131 Hollywood Blvd., Suite 403
Hollywood, FL 33020
phone: (954) 589-0628
website: www.theiai.org

The world's oldest and largest forensic science identification association, the International Association for Identification has more than sixty-five hundred members from seventy-seven countries. By accessing the Resources link on the group's website, visitors can read postings for job openings in forensic science.

International Crime Scene Investigators Association

15774 S. LaGrange Rd.
Orland Park, IL 60462
phone: (708) 460-8082
Website: http://icsia.org

The International Crime Scene Investigators Association provides general information on the science of forensic investigation to police departments that may need the skills of a forensic science technician. Information on pursuing a career as a forensic science technician can be found on the group's website by accessing the link for How to Become a CSI.

Pharmacy Technician

A Growing Field

Drug stores as well as hospitals and other health care providers hire pharmacy technicians to perform several tasks, freeing up pharmacists to concentrate more on their duties to formulate and package medications in the proper dosages. Among the duties that have been shifted to pharmacy technicians are counting out the correct number of pills required for particular prescriptions; talking to customers by phone; packaging and labeling prescriptions; inputting customer information into the pharmacy's computer database; organizing the pharmacy's inventory; and carrying out orders from the pharmacists who supervise them.

In recent years, pharmacy technicians have found their services much in demand due to the aging baby boomer population as well as adoption of the Affordable Care Act—a 2010 federal law which strives to guarantee affordable health care to virtually all Americans. As a result of the law, more people are using pharmacies than ever before. That translates to more work than the average pharmacist can handle on his or her own. Pharmacy technicians are

A pharmacy technician answers a customer's questions about her prescription. Pharmacy technicians talk to customers, help fill prescriptions, assist with customer databases, and organize inventory.

taking up a lot of the slack. Although they earn considerably less than pharmacists (who typically earn about $121,500 a year), pharmacy technicians are nevertheless highly valued by their employers. In a busy pharmacy, technicians need to carry out their duties quickly, accurately, and with a positive attitude—even when some of the customers are cranky, impatient, and unhappy as they wait for their prescriptions to be filled. For the right individuals the job of helping people get their medicine, and to feel better when they get well, can be highly satisfying.

Using Your Math and Science Skills

Pharmacy technicians need strong math and science skills. Lessons you were taught in your middle school and high school classes on the metric system will be important resources if you choose a career as a pharmacy technician. In this job, grams and liters are standard measurements. Your knowledge of chemistry, anatomy, and physiology would also help you do your job.

For example, Jonathan Roach, a certified pharmacy technician, says prospective pharmacy technicians should learn all they can about the way medications they dispense work in the body. Also, prospective pharmacy technicians would do well to understand how medications are concocted by the pharmaceutical companies. They will learn all that by studying pharmacology. A fundamental lesson taught to future pharmacy technicians focuses on what type of medications are prescribed for specific ailments. Further, he says that pharmacy technicians should know as much as possible about doses and side effects and toxicity of medications. That knowledge is obtained by studying a subject known as therapeutics.

Roach, who teaches pharmacy technician courses at Cuyahoga Community College in Cleveland, Ohio, authored a chapter in the textbook *Understanding Pharmacology for Pharmacy Technicians*. He writes:

> Familiarity with the physical and chemical properties of a drug contributes to the ability to choose the right way to handle and prepare it for use by a physician or patient. It helps the technician understand why a drug is stored in the refrigerator, protected from exposure to light, or kept in a specialized section of the pharmacy (like the ones for emergency medications, hazardous drugs, or controlled substances). Having studied pharmacology, the technician has a better grasp of which drugs are usually taken by mouth, which drugs are injected, and which ones are applied directly to the part of the body where they should have an effect, and thus the technician can assist the pharmacist more effectively.

Where Pharmacy Technicians Work

More than half of all pharmacy technicians are employed in small independent drugstores or large chains like Walgreens, Rite Aid, or CVS. Many pharmacy technicians find work in large supermarkets

Typical Day in a Mail-Order Pharmacy

"In a mail-order pharmacy, there are a variety of different work areas—some are more specialized than others. I am fortunate enough to have been trained to handle the responsibilities particular to most of the areas of the pharmacy, so my day has the potential to be filled with a variety of different tasks. Daily duties for Mail-Order Pharmacy Technicians can range from filling individual vials to replenishing large dispensing cells, preparing medications and compounds, and entering patient and prescription information into the pharmacy's database. It's a fast-paced environment with a high expectation on quality that requires an individual with an exceptional attention to detail and the ability to work under pressure."

Evan Phillips, quoted in Arizona College, "Day in the Life of a Pharmacy Technician." www.arizonacollege.edu.

and department stores, such as Wegmans or Walmart, which provide pharmacy services to their customers. Others find work in hospitals, which employ technicians in their in-house pharmacies.

Pharmacy technicians are also employed by the military, which needs skilled people to assist veterans and active-duty personnel in military hospitals and clinics. Some pharmacy technicians may even work on US Navy ships or in military field hospitals.

The best wages can be found in hospital employment. Getting a job in a hospital is more difficult than getting a job in a retail pharmacy. Hospitals are more selective in whom they hire because hospital pharmacy technicians are required to do more. Hospital pharmacies tend to provide a higher volume of prescriptions to their patients per day than retail pharmacies. This means hospital pharmacy technicians are busier and under more pressure than pharmacy technicians employed in retail establishments. In addition, hospital pharmacy technicians work under less supervision than their peers in the retail sector and are responsible for reading patient medical charts and making notes in the charts.

In an essay describing elements of her job written for the website Pharmacytechpros.com, Chicago hospital pharmacy technician Michelle Goeking explains,

> The pharmacy has little direct contact with patients, but does most of its communication with the nurses or physicians on staff by telephone or electronically. Medication orders usually come to the pharmacy through a fax machine, pneumatic tube system, or more recently, electronically. Some inpatient pharmacy facilities allow pharmacy technicians to input these orders, but all facilities require the pharmacy technician to fill medications for these orders. Technicians in these facilities also must be able to interpret medical orders and perform pharmacy calculations related to the job. Technology has played a huge role in the institutional pharmacy setting, so a pharmacy technician in this capacity will be trained to fill and troubleshoot the automated medication dispensers found in patient areas.

Because hospitals require a greater variety of medications to treat very sick patients, their pharmacy technicians need to know how to formulate those medications. That might mean actually creating them from their component chemicals in a process called compounding. They may also help create intravenous (IV) solutions—liquefied medications that are administered to a patient through a needle connected to a tube and plastic bag. These medications are administered through a patient's veins rather than taken by mouth. Another difference is that hospital pharmacy technicians have no contact with customers: The medications they provide will be dispensed to nurses, who in turn will see that their patients take them.

Qualifications Needed

Unlike most jobs in the health care industry, pharmacy technicians don't need extensive education. Training may be strictly on the job or obtained through vocational school, through the military, or by enrolling in a community college. Such training usually takes no more than a year, including time for clinical experience.

Hospitals generally hire techs who have a few years' experience and who have passed certification exams. Such exams are given by the Pharmacy Technician Certification Board. Passing the test enables technicians to earn the designation certified pharmacy technician, or CPhT.

Advancement

If you would want to make yourself even more valuable as a pharmacy technician you could find opportunities to specialize. Technicians can take Internet-based courses on their home computers in such specialties as sterile products and compounding. Sterile products include eye drops and IV solutions that must be produced in very clean environments because of the dangers of infection and contamination. Compounding classes teach students how to put together medications that don't require sterile environments. Students learn all about ointments, gels, capsules, powders, drops, and suspensions as well as aspects of quality control and record keeping.

Students may also take courses in the handling of chemotherapy drugs that are used to treat cancer patients. Chemotherapy drugs often include many harsh chemicals that kill human cells and therefore must be handled with great care. Chemotherapy training teaches students how to handle these drugs, covering protective devices and proper disposal of the drugs among other topics.

Similarly, about 1 percent of pharmacy technicians work in nuclear pharmacies, which also focus on cancer treatment. The nuclear pharmaceutical field is considered a growing specialty. The radioactive materials dispensed by these pharmacies are used in radiation treatments, which kill cancerous cells as well as other human cells. Since nuclear pharmacy technicians (NPTs) can be expected to work with hazardous substances, these specialized technicians need to be educated about how to compound these

Using Your Math Skills

"You will need a firm grasp on several measurement systems—especially the metric, avoirdupois and apothecary systems. The apothecary system is used for measuring some thyroid drugs and aspirin. The avoirdupois system is commonly used for prepackaged or bulk medications. Drug doses are typically given in milligrams, grams or milliliters, so you'll use the metric system most often. You'll also need to know how to convert prescriptions between measurement systems. Pharmacy computer systems use metric measurements for medication doses, for example, but prescriptions are often given to customers in ounces, teaspoons, or drops."

Melissa King, "What Math Do You Need to Know to Become a Pharmacists Tech?," Demand Media. http://classroom.synonym.com.

medicines without exposing themselves and others to dangerous degrees of radiation. One way they minimize their exposure is by compounding products while shielding themselves behind glass barriers.

Thomas J. Foley, an NPT from Chicago, described elements of his job in an essay on the website Triadisotopes.com, which is sponsored by his employer, Triad Isotopes, which develops radiation treatments for cancer patients. Says Foley,

Many NPTs are attracted to the profession due to the hands-on experience they receive working with radioactive material and the vital service they provide to patients in need of diagnosis or therapy. At least that is how it is for me. Many of my colleagues also find the workplace atmosphere of a nuclear pharmacy to be more desirable than the common community pharmacy, because of the specialized nature and significance of patient care involved.

Foley added, though, that the working hours can be unusual. For an NPT, the day usually starts at 2 a.m. due to the preparation time it takes to make radiation therapy drugs available to patients during normal daytime hours. He says, "In those wee hours of the morning, technicians work alongside pharmacists to draw most of the patient doses."

Future Prospects

People who are thinking about careers as pharmacy technicians will be positioning themselves for careers that are growing faster than average. Jobs are expected to grow by 9 percent through 2024. In 2014, the average salary for pharmacy technicians was $29,810. An average of $34,640 was earned by technicians working in hospitals. How much money you can make also depends on the state where you work. According to the *U.S. News & World Report* website, the highest wages can be found in California—particularly in San Francisco, San Jose, Napa, Santa Rosa, and Santa Cruz. *U.S. News & World Report* is a news site that frequently ranks colleges, hospitals, occupations, and other areas of interest to consumers.

Find Out More

American Association of Pharmacy Technicians
PO Box 1447
Greensboro, NC 27402
phone: (336) 333-4771
website: www.pharmacytechnician.com

The American Association of Pharmacy Technicians provides continuing education opportunities to its members and helps them to find jobs and keep up with current trends in the profession. By accessing the link for Career Center on the group's website, visitors can find postings for jobs listing the duties the technicians are expected to perform.

American Pharmacists Association
2215 Constitution Ave. NW
Washington, DC 20037
phone: (202) 628-4410
website: www.pharmacist.com

The American Pharmacists Association has more than sixty thousand members comprising pharmacy technicians, pharmacists, pharmaceutical scientists, and student pharmacists. It offers a career center and reference center and assists people in the pharmacy industry to learn and practice more effectively.

American Society of Health-System Pharmacists (ASHP)
7272 Wisconsin Ave.
Bethesda, MD 20814
phone: (866) 279-0681
website: www.ashp.org

This organization develops standards by which pharmacists and pharmacy technicians are expected to perform their jobs. Visitors to the ASHP website can find many resources explaining the jobs of pharmacists and pharmacy technicians, including webinars devoted to guiding members through new standards and practices in their professions.

National Pharmacy Technician Association
PO Box 683148
Houston, TX 77268
phone: (888) 247-8700
website: www.pharmacytechnician.org

The largest professional organization for pharmacy technicians, the National Pharmacy Technician Association's members work in retail, independent, hospital, mail-order, home care, long-term care, nuclear, military, correctional facility, and academic locations. The association provides classes, certifies technicians, and produces the bimonthly magazine *Today's Technician*.

Physician Assistant

A Few Facts

Number of Jobs
As of 2014, 94,400

Salaries
As of 2014, the average salary is $95,820.

Educational Requirements
Master's degree

Personal Qualities
Problem solver, good communicator, team player

Work Setting
Inside physician's offices and in hospitals

Future Job Outlook
Job growth of 30 percent through 2024, which is much faster than average

Helping Patients Achieve Better Health

Here's a riddle: You can prescribe medicine, examine patients, diagnose their ailments, and educate them on healthy living practices and disease management. What are you? If you answered "doctor" you're right but here's something worth knowing: This also describes the job of a physician assistant, or PA. PAs do just about everything physicians do, except that their work must be supervised by a doctor. But that doesn't mean they would have a physician standing over them all the time. To the contrary, they spend much of their days working independently, perhaps meeting with their superiors once a day to talk over cases. Kimberly Mackey works as a physician assistant in a clinic in Houston, Texas. In an essay written for the website of the American Academy of Physician Assistants, Mackey said,

> I enjoy being a physician assistant because my work is challenging, yet very rewarding. I am able to practice medicine within a multidisciplinary team

where I consult with my supervising physicians daily. . . . In our clinic, PAs are able to see patients and perform procedures with a high level of independence, which is what I like about the clinic setting. I see patients on my own schedule, but may always consult with one of my supervising physicians if I have any questions.

Skill Set Needed

If physician assistant sounds like a job you'd want to do, you'll also want to consider the traits and skills needed for this kind of work. You should be sensitive to other people's pain and discomfort. You should be compassionate. You should be good at explaining complex concepts in simple terms. You should be willing to work well with others. And, of course, you should have an interest in medicine and its related sciences, such as biology and chemistry.

PAs work closely with physicians but also have to manage the care of patients. Therefore, PAs must be capable of working independently. PAs have physicians backing them up but must

A Satisfying Career

"I realized that what I wanted most out of life was to help people be healthy. I love the human body, I love anatomy and I love science. I loved the thought of propping a young child up on the exam room table making a funny face and treating their ear infection. I loved the idea of sewing up a wound, setting a fracture, being there when another human being needed someone to hold onto. Helping someone come to terms with death while helping another come to terms with life. I didn't want MD, I wanted all of the above; to me there was no other way [than to be a physician assistant]."

Stephen Pasquini, "Why My Wife Is Happy I Am a Physician Assistant and Not an MD," *PA Life* (blog). www.thepalife.com.

be able to do significant caseload work on their own, freeing the doctor to do other tasks. As such, a PA must have the ability to stay calm and focused during emergencies and periods of high stress. PAs have to be able to respond appropriately when crises occur. "I see patients both independently and in conjunction with my supervising surgeon," says Bianca Belcher, a physician assistant in Boston, Massachusetts. "These appointments can range from a new patient coming for an initial evaluation to a post-operative patient that needs their [stitches] removed. I perform physical exams, review imaging, explain procedures, obtain consent for upcoming surgeries, write notes, and coordinate care with other services such as family medicine, oncology, neurology, and the pain service." Belcher, who works as a PA in a practice that focuses on neurosurgery— surgical treatment of diseases of the brain and spine—is the author of an essay on the duties of a physician assistant written for the website GradSchools.com.

How They Spend Their Days

Workdays for physician assistants vary according to the area of medicine in which they work. For example, a PA who works in orthopedic surgery, which focuses on diseases and injuries to muscles and bones, might spend part of his or her day in an operating room assisting the surgeon. Other parts of the day may involve treating a patient in the office with an injection to ease knee pain, ordering an X-ray for another patient, and trying to determine what is causing another patient's ankle pain.

A PA who works in family medicine may have a far different schedule. That health care provider might see patients as young as newborns to patients who are elderly for a variety of health concerns. The PA might spend time talking with the supervising physician about the patients who would be coming in, ordering X-rays, looking over blood test results, and treating another patient's bleeding wound by sewing a row of stitches with a sterile needle and surgical thread. "Every day brings new challenges," says Michael Evans, a physician assistant who works in family medicine

45

Flexible but Sometimes Frustrating

"I love being a PA, practicing medicine and making a difference. I would not change what I do. This does not mean that there are not days when I am frustrated, angered or annoyed with being a PA. But I love the flexibility; I have worked the typical 40-hour week and I have worked the nights/days/weekends/holiday schedules. No matter what turn my life takes I can find a PA job to fit it. I love that I can have a crazy day in the [intensive care unit] . . . and at the end of the day I go home."

Jennifer Nowacyk, quoted in Jessi Rodriguez Ohanesian, *The Ultimate Guide to the Physician Assistant Profession*. New York: McGraw-Hill Education, 2013, p. 14.

at the University of Utah's Stansbury Park Health Center. "I get to meet new people and help them with anything from depression to sinus infections, to back pain, diabetes management, headaches [and] abdominal pain. Just when I think that I have heard every possible complaint someone will surprise me with an off the wall complaint that really makes me think." Evans wrote about his job for a website maintained by the University of Utah.

Getting into PA School

The profession of physician assistant is growing, which means that college PA programs (which are graduate-level programs) have become highly competitive. Some experts even recommend applying to up to twelve schools to increase the chance of getting accepted to one of them. Mary Jo Wiemiller of Marquette University College of Health Science in Milwaukee, Wisconsin, told *U.S. News & World Report* that Marquette's PA school can, at best, accept just 10 percent of those who apply. She said, "With heightened awareness of the PA profession in the last decade, it has become increasingly more competitive to gain acceptance to a PA training program."

Physician assistant programs have many requirements. One is a bachelor's degree in life sciences, which involves courses such as organic chemistry, microbiology, and anatomy. Most of the more than two hundred PA schools in the United States also require candidates for admission to have worked anywhere from eighty to two thousand hours in the health care field. That's a big reason most PAs are at least twenty-seven years old before they start working in the field. The type of experience required by PA programs may include hours spent working as an emergency medical technician (EMT), a professional who provides emergency care to accident victims and others who experience traumatic injuries, often as a member of an ambulance crew. A PA school would also accept a candidate who works as a paramedic—a job similar to that of an EMT, but with a higher level of training and skill set. Experience as a nurse would qualify a candidate for admission to a PA program. So would experience as a nurse's assistant or physical therapy aide. "We really are looking for—and I think a lot of other programs are, too—students who've had some previous healthcare experience where they've had some direct interactions with patients," says David P. Asprey, director of the physician assistant program at the University of Iowa Carver College of Medicine. "[It] adds a level of maturity." Asprey made those comments in an interview with *U.S. News & World Report*.

If you're considering a career as a physician assistant you don't actually have to wait until college to get some experience. With training, you can begin working as an EMT as early as age eighteen. It's also possible to join a junior EMT program at age fourteen.

What Is PA School Like?

Once enrolled in PA programs students will learn many of the same subjects medical students learn but in less depth. As with medical students, they will also participate in hands-on health care through rotations in such areas as pediatrics, surgery, obstetrics and gynecology, emergency medicine, psychiatry, internal medicine, and geriatrics. Rotations provide opportunities to participate in clinical settings and to begin thinking about which areas seem to carry the most interest for the student PA. Students typically spend one or two months in each rotation. Kelly Moylen, who is studying to be a PA at the University of Utah in Salt Lake City, described what going to PA school is like for a website maintained by her university. Asked to describe a typical day at PA school she replied:

> We are typically in school Monday through Friday, from 8 to 5. So it's like a full-time job. We do get an hour at lunch to go outside and run or keep studying. Whatever kind of works for you. You're up early and you're at school and your brain is firing all day long. And then you come home and you just kind of got to keep with it and it goes all night long as well and it's just one day at a time.

The typical PA program lasts for two years. During that time students will need to absorb a tremendous amount of information. Moylen says, "It's like mini-medical school. . . . We go for two years constantly, no summers off, all day long, and it is everything shoved in really quickly. So really taking all that in and being able to process it knowing like I need to know this stuff. I don't just need to memorize it."

Robustly Healthy Prognosis

If a medical career appeals to you, but not the long trajectory of medical school plus post-graduate residency experience, a career as a physician assistant could be just right—especially since the future prospects for the career look very bright. Physician assistant jobs are expected to grow 30 percent through 2024—a growth not seen in many other professions. Salaries for PAs are also good. For physician assistants who work in doctors' offices, the average salary is $95,820 a year. You could make even more if you work in an outpatient care center ($100,750) or a hospital ($99,360).

Providing Personal Attention

"PAs are able to spend more time with the patient in a clinic than a physician, which is something I am always happy to do, and frankly is the aspect of the job that appeals to me most. I enjoy educating my patients [about diseases]. . . . I feel this gives the patient a deeper understanding of their healthcare. Physicians often do not have time for such personal attention and patient education due to overbooked schedules, so PAs take pride in this aspect of the job."

Jordan Hall, quoted in Lifehacker, "Career Spotlight: What I Do as a Physician Assistant," May 19, 2015. http://lifehacker.com.

That robust growth for physician assistant jobs is mainly due to the implementation of the Affordable Care Act in 2014, which helped make medical care more affordable for millions of Americans. Many medical practices have been swamped with new patients, requiring doctors to try new strategies for patient care. One of these is the use of physician assistants. Says Wiemiller, "Ten years ago when I introduced myself patients would ask, 'What's a PA?' Now, when treating patients, they respond with something like, 'Oh, my niece or nephew is in PA school.'"

Find Out More

American Academy of Physician Assistants (AAPA)
2318 Mill Rd., Suite 1300
Alexandria, VA 22314
phone: (703) 836-2272
website: www.aapa.org

The AAPA represents more than 108,500 certified PAs across the country. Its membership includes students. The organization keeps members abreast of the latest news in the profession, offers an online community for PAs to network, and produces the monthly *Journal of American Academy of Physician Assistants*.

National Commission on Certification of Physician Assistants
12000 Findley Rd., Suite 100
Johns Creek, GA 30094
phone: (678) 417-8100
website: www.nccpa.net

Since it was started in 1975, the National Commission on Certification of Physician Assistants has certified more than 111,000 physician assistants. The organization's website offers information on who is eligible to be certified and provides information on the Physician Assistant National Certifying Examination. Also offered is a statistical profile of its members.

Physician Assistant Education Association
655 K St. NW, Suite 700
Washington, DC 20001
phone: (703) 548 5538
website: http://paeaonline.org

As the national organization representing physician assistant education programs in the United States, the Physician Assistant Education Association collects, publishes, and disseminates information on PA programs. Its website offers resources for prospective students including a blog, school directory, and instructions on how to submit a single application to multiple schools.

Physician Assistant Life
website: www.thepalife.com

Physician Assistant Life is a blog written by family practice physician assistant Stephen Pasquini, who has thirteen years of clinical experience. Pasquini provides such resources as a podcast study guide for certification, as well as posts on the pros and cons of entering the profession.

Robotics Engineer

Solving Human Problems

Robotics engineering is a cutting-edge field in which professionals design robots to perform chores that humans otherwise prefer not to do or are unable to do. Robots perform chores that may be too mundane, such as welding the same parts over and over again onto the chassis of new cars in an automobile factory. Or these jobs may be disagreeable—robots armed with cameras have been inserted into sewage pipes to search for leaks. Or these jobs might be dangerous: Many police departments employ robots to inspect suspicious packages or pieces of luggage that may contain bombs. The military also makes wide use of robots, employing them as drones, which fly over terrorist cells, photographing their activities or launching missiles to wipe them out.

Moreover, there are also many jobs performed by robots that are truly on the frontiers of technology. Robots are used by the National Aeronautics and Space Administration (NASA) in space exploration—robots have already ambled across the surface of Mars looking for evidence of life. Oceanographers wishing to probe below the seas farther than human beings can safely go use robots. So do surgeons who may not even be in the same country as the person receiving the operation. In addition, it is likely that in your lifetime you will be a passenger in a self-driving car guided by robotics. Imagine it—this could totally eliminate the human error that leads to countless automobile accidents, fatalities, and injuries.

These robots do not resemble the popular notion of a "mechanical man"—popularized in science fiction—that looks human, walks on two legs, and even communicates verbally. Rather, these robots are configured in all manner of shapes and sizes but they all have one important trait in common: They can be programmed to carry out many different functions, remotely guided by humans or computers.

Robotics engineers don't just design robots. They also maintain them and troubleshoot the devices if they malfunction, conduct research on new ways robots can be used, and write the software that tells the computers that run the robots what to do. In an interview posted on NASA's website, robotics engineer Ann Morfopoulos says,

> I love seeing things that work. I was always driven to try and find a way to apply an abstract theory or equation to physical phenomena I could observe. . . . In robotics, the goal is always toward application—the robot should work better or have some new capability after you have designed a new piece of technology. Robotics is so broad, requiring mechanical, electrical and computer science.

Helpful Traits

People who design robots are proficient in mathematics. They have also acquired the skills needed to write software. They think creatively, find new ways to solve problems, and tune in to other people's needs to help guide them in designing robots that perform specific functions. They harbor a curiosity about how

Exploring Under the Sea

"If I had to describe a 'typical' day, it would include some project development/proposal writing (bringing in new work and new imagining capabilities), testing and integrating sensor packages on autonomous underwater vehicles like cameras, sonar and many other oceanographic sensors, then testing them in the waters of Cape Cod in preparation for an expedition somewhere in the world. Several times a year I travel and lead expeditions ranging from under-ice operations, fish and scallop surveys and even many Navy projects."

Amy Kukulya, quoted in EngineerGirl, "Amy Kukulya Interview," June 15, 2015. www .engineergirl.org.

things work and are very good at taking apart—and putting back together—machines as they figure out why something isn't working as it should.

Amy Kukulya designs undersea robots for the Woods Hole Oceanographic Institution in Woods Hole, Massachusetts. It is the world's largest ocean research, engineering, and education organization. Writing on the website EngineerGirl, which is maintained by the National Academy of Engineering, Kukulya explains the need for robotics engineers to be well rounded:

It is not enough to build a robot, but it is important and a lot more fun if you can understand the applications of what you are creating. For example, I work with robots that explore our oceans. My team is constantly improving our technology by using robots in conjunction with scientists who we specifically design them for. If a scientist wants to be able to take photos in 6,000 meters of dark, turbid waters of a shipwreck, we need to design a system that can swim that deep and take pictures using flashes and that can navigate blindly.

Since robots are, after all, machines, many robotics engineers are good at the hands-on business of making a machine run. In other words, they know how to wield a screwdriver and other tools. Kukulya says she is at home using a soldering iron—a small tool that employs heat to permanently fuse pieces together. She also uses an oscilloscope, a device for testing electronic equipment by measuring fluctuations in electrical current.

Becoming a Robotics Professional

Robotics engineers generally earn BS degrees in robotics engineering. Many go on to earn master's degrees and doctorates. However, you can work in the field with a degree in mechanical, manufacturing, electrical, or software engineering. The reason there is so much leeway is that people from all of those fields are needed to handle the various components of making robots function properly. In basic terms mechanical engineers are experts in the physical aspects of the robot's body. Electrical engineers specialize in the electrical circuits that enable the commands to be received by the robot. Software engineers focus on the computer code that directs the robot's tasks. Also, software engineers are exploring the new field of artificial intelligence in which more sophisticated robots are able to react to situations without specifically being programmed to do so. They are, to some degree, replicating human thinking.

Regardless of whether students major specifically in robotics engineering or in one of the related engineering fields, among the subjects they will probably study are hydraulics and pneumatics—the use of water, oil, or other fluids to provide pressure within the machine's components, enabling the robot to move. They may also study how to design and manufacture robots and their components using computer-aided design and computer-aided manufacturing programs called CAD/CAM.

Marcia O'Malley, associate professor of mechanical engineering and materials science at Rice University in Houston, Texas, described the value of such an education from an employer's point of view. She told the *Houston Chronicle* newspaper,

Mechanical and robotic engineering students learn how to approach a problem, generate solutions, evaluate solutions and support their decisions with engineering fundamentals. Robotics students gain additional training in system integration—making the computer control work with the sensors and electronics, and the mechanical system, all coordinated together. This level of integration requires interdisciplinary knowledge, which is a strength of those trained in robotics.

Higher degrees provide opportunities to take on more responsibilities. With a master's degree robotics engineers can develop robots, work on research, and find work as a design project manager. With a doctorate degree they can pursue higher levels of research and development and teach engineering students at the college level.

How You Can Explore Robotics Now

You don't have to wait for college to explore robotics. Many schools and community groups sponsor clubs that enable people with the same interests in robotics to work on common projects together. Building a robot is a team effort, even on a professional level, so getting some hands-on experience with other enthusiastic people is an excellent introduction to what could lead to an exciting career.

Jim Arndt, a science teacher at Martinsburg High School in Martinsburg, West Virginia, is the faculty adviser for the school's robotics club. In 2016, the club's members fashioned robots out of LEGO bricks that they could control with their tablet computers. (The components for the robots were contained in LEGO EV3 kits, which the toymaker has designed for young robotics students.) "This club gives the students the opportunity to learn programming and problem solving. I let the kids do all the work, and I just give them the place to do it. These robots are their creation," Arndt said in an interview with the *Journal News* newspaper in

Martinsburg. "Robotics is a hands-on, tangible application of STEM [science, technology, engineering, and math] skills, and [the students] love it."

There are also competitions to enter, such as the FIRST Robotics Competition, now more than twenty-five years old. The competition is sponsored by the organization For Inspiration and Recognition of Science and Technology (FIRST), a nonprofit group based in Manchester, New Hampshire. Some seventy-five thousand high school students from around the world participate each year. The competition is open to students of all technical abilities and consists of teams of ten or more students working with two adult mentors.

Another option is to pursue a summer internship in robotics available to high school students. Many universities, government agencies, and private companies offer such internships. Among the organizations that seek interns in robotics are electronics firm Apple, aerospace company Boeing, and NASA.

In addition to striving to get hands-on experience with robotics, high school students would do well to select classes providing them with solid foundations to study engineering in college.

The Thrill of Robotics

"I love my job at JPL [NASA Jet Propulsion Lab], where I get to design, build and test robots. I get to use nearly everything I learned in school to do my job, and there are always new challenges involved where I continuously get to read and learn even more. I also get to work with a lot of very smart, creative and exciting people who are willing to teach me what they know and work with me on different projects. Most of all, I love getting the chance to come up with new ideas for how to explore space, the solar system, and beyond."

Paulo Younse, quoted in Imaginverse Educational Consortium, "An Interview with Paulo Younse," May 19, 2006. www.imagiverse.org.

These courses include physics, chemistry, geometry, algebra, calculus, and computer science. Many high schools have also established classes in robotics.

Future Prospects in Robotics

Given its status as a cutting-edge field whose members are highly skilled and highly educated, the profession of robotics engineer is expected to see growth. According to the Bureau of Labor Statistics, the profession is expected to grow by about 6 percent by 2020. "Today there are more opportunities than ever before in the robotics industry," says Jeff Burnstein, president of the Ann Arbor, Michigan, industry trade group Robotics Industries Association (RIA). Quoted in a 2016 RIA press release, he says, "The continuing growth in robotics is opening many new job opportunities for people who can program, install, run and maintain robots."

Salaries for robotics engineers are also quite good. In 2012, robotics engineers earned average salaries of $90,580. One university that tracks the employment status of its graduates is Worcester Polytechnic Institute of Worcester, Massachusetts. According to the school's website, graduates with master's degrees in robotics engineering can expect to earn average salaries of $110,000 a year.

A new entrant into the field is Rhys Isaac, who at age twenty-three is a trainee robot engineer for a company in Wales in Great Britain. He is thrilled to be working on a prototype for a miniature battlefield drone that has four rotors. Isaac majored in computer science and electronics at Swansea University in Wales. "It's very hard to recruit employees with the right combination of theoretical engineering knowledge and practical skills," his supervisor, Barry Davies, told the *Telegraph*, a London-based daily newspaper, in 2014. "People like Rhys are going to be in big demand."

Find Out More

National Aeronautics and Space Administration (NASA) Robotics Alliance Project
website: http://robotics.nasa.gov

NASA's project was formed to foster a continuing interest in robotic space exploration missions. A section for students highlights summer camps and internships, information about artificial intelligence, robotic challenges, and colleges that feature robotics programs.

Robotics Industries Association (RIA)
900 Victors Way, Suite 140
Ann Arbor, MI 48108
phone: (734) 994-6088
website: www.robotics.org

The RIA is a trade group serving the robotics industry. Members include leading robot manufacturers, users, system integrators, component suppliers, research groups, and consulting firms. The RIA holds conferences and keeps statistics on the robotics industry.

Science Trek
website: http://idahoptv.org

Science Trek is a web and broadcast project of Idaho Public Television. It explores science, technology, engineering, and mathematics topics. A page on robotics discusses the history of robots, artificial intelligence, tiny robots, and robot parts.

SME
1 SME Dr.
Dearborn, MI 48121
phone: (800) 733-4763
website: www.sme.org

Formerly known as the Society of Manufacturing Engineers, SME is a nonprofit organization dedicated to the needs of advanced manufacturing and preparing the skilled workforce to meet future needs. Student members can find information on manufacturing processes and networking opportunities.

Science Educator

Producing Tomorrow's Scientists

If you look forward to your classes in biology, chemistry, and physics, and you think the people who teach those classes are cool, you may want to consider a career in which you too would have the opportunity to teach the sciences to young people. If you accept that career choice, you could find opportunities at many levels—from middle schools, where teens are given their first in-depth educations in the sciences, to university graduate programs, where future PhDs earn their diplomas.

In his 2011 State of the Union address, President Barack Obama set a goal of preparing 100,000 teachers by 2021 in the so-called STEM fields, which include science, technology, engineering, and mathematics. So there is national momentum to produce more science educators, and that is leading to robust predictions for job growth in the field. Moreover, by becoming a science educator you could play a role in the future of industrial development, medical breakthroughs, and other scientific discoveries by helping to educate young people who would go on to careers in the sciences. In their book *Methods of Teaching Science*, university science professors Kandi Jaya Sree and Digumarti Bhaskara Rao provide this advice to prospective science teachers:

> Science is like a key that opens doors everywhere—on the bottom of the ocean, with the astronauts in space, with the plants, animals, and man here on earth, with thousands of conveniences of our daily lives. Learning about science . . . stretches your mind, but gives you a lot in return. You always have something new to bring to your classes. And you as a science teacher have many satisfactions that come from working with young students.

What Kind of Person Makes a Good Science Teacher?

Teaching general science, biology, physics, earth science, or chemistry requires mastery of the subject matter. In fact, science teachers have to do more than understand what they are teaching: They have to transfer the material to their students by the force of their enthusiasm, personalities, and ability to relate to the students. They also need to design experiments and other activities that enhance what students learn from class handouts and textbooks. Bunsen burners, microscopes, generators, test tubes, chemicals, and other resources are employed.

Being a science teacher means being able to excite the sleepy faces of students early in the morning. And at the end of the day, the science teacher must also find a way to capture the interests of bored students who are already thinking about what they might do after school. It requires having the ability to put students' needs ahead of your own, to give them whatever they need to understand the material you are trying to convey, and, when necessary, to be a disciplinarian.

You will probably want to be the sort of teacher Emma Alice Miller had while attending Santa Monica High School in California.

The High of Teaching

"Science takes my breath away! I become someone else when I talk about it. I thoroughly enjoy mind-mapping its details, and communicating them to an expectant crowd of middle-schoolers has far exceeded any corporate presentation I've ever done. The high, in the classroom, is unreal!"

Maggie Bolado, quoted in Concordia University–Portland, "Science Teacher Career: Job, Education and Salary Information," October 15, 2014. http://education.cu-portland.edu.

Miller planned to study physics in college because her teacher, Mrs. Reardon, made it seem like fun. "For a unit on motion, we dropped water balloons and timed them, and then did calculations on this data. Mrs. Reardon was able to get everyone in the class to participate," Miller told the *Hechinger Report*, a journal for educators.

What Science Teachers Do

Having sat in science classes yourself, you may think you already have a good idea of what science teachers do. You may recall that in elementary school your science teacher may also have been your math teacher, social studies teacher, and English teacher. Elementary school teachers are responsible for teaching many subjects during the course of the school day. They have to carefully adhere to a curriculum set by their school district and the state.

It is in middle school, therefore, where students first encounter teachers who are devoted solely to teaching science. Likewise, when students arrive in high school they find science teachers as well. Homing in on particular areas such as physics, biology, and chemistry, teachers cover these topics in greater depth with older students. Middle school and high school science teachers may also guide students participating in science fair competitions.

These are extracurricular activities that allow students to compete for recognition with students from other schools in projects they choose themselves.

Perhaps the biggest way science teachers shape students is influencing how they look at the world. Middle school chemistry teacher Hans de Grys said he views his job as teaching students how to think. "I know that 98 percent of them won't remember that HF [hydrofluoric acid] is a weak acid, or what effective nuclear charge is," he said. "And that's OK. I hope that they learn and remember how to attack a tough problem or how to be comfortable with ambiguity. I hope they learn how to plan an investigation, how to analyze data, and how to check and see if an answer makes sense. I hope they become both thoughtful and skeptical, in the best sense of those words. I hope that they learn to collaborate effectively with their peers, deal productively with setbacks, and gain confidence in themselves." De Grys was interviewed by the website Branching Points, a career guidance site for university science students.

There are some significant differences between teaching in high schools or middle schools and teaching in university classrooms. High school and middle school teachers usually have to

Meticulous Preparation

"Teaching is a wonderful combination of science and interpersonal interactions. The best part of the job is inspiring young minds by sharing my joy and wonder for science. The time in front of the classroom is the easiest and most fun part of the day, but a good lesson requires meticulous preparation. A typical day begins with arriving early and making sure the classroom is prepared for the day's activities. Science teaching differs from many other disciplines due to the extra effort involved in preparing a laboratory intensive experience for students."

Mike Zito, quoted in *Science Teacher*, "Career of the Month," September 2006, p. 84.

use textbooks and other materials that administrators select for the schools. On a university level, teachers can pick their own textbooks or even elect not to use them. University-level teachers also have responsibilities that go beyond the classroom. They are responsible for researching developments in their fields then publishing articles and books about their research. They must also work one-on-one with students who are studying for advanced degrees, serving as mentors while their students work toward their PhDs.

Anyone considering being a science teacher should know that teachers usually put in more hours than the typical American worker does. According to a 2012 report called *Primary Sources: America's Teachers on the Teaching Profession*, the average teacher works fifty-three hours a week—nearly eleven hours a day. So if you want to be a science teacher you can expect that you would not be headed home the minute the 3 p.m. bell rings. More likely, you would stay an hour or more after school to help students before going home to spend another ninety-five minutes or so grading tests and preparing for the next day's labs and classroom lessons.

How Do You Train to Be a Teacher?

To be a science teacher you need to be a graduate of a four-year college, typically with a bachelor's degree in science education. Such a degree is granted when students master not only the science concepts needed for their major but also the courses that pertain to being educators. Science teachers who earn master's degrees will earn more money than those who lack graduate degrees. Meanwhile, to teach on the college level a doctorate in science education is expected in order to earn a tenured position. Professors with tenure have greater protection from layoffs and firings.

Not everyone who becomes a teacher studied to do so in college. An alternative path that can lead to a teaching job is through Teach for America, a program that has placed more than fifty thousand college graduates into two-year teaching positions in schools in urban and rural areas where most students are living in poverty. To apply for the program, you need a college degree with a grade point average that is 2.5 or higher (with 4.0 being all A's). New corps members, as they are called, learn to teach on the job, receiving feedback from experienced teachers as well as assistance with their lesson plans.

Teach for America also offers fellowships, which are opportunities for future educators to take workshops to boost their science knowledge. Shaundra Miller, a fifth-grade teacher in Richmond, Virginia, was awarded one of the fellowships. That enabled her to be more effective at teaching science since her college education lacked a science focus. "Many teachers don't actually know much about science and they need to feel empowered before they can teach. It wasn't until I had the training that I was able to try it," she said in an interview with the education website For Richmond.

Job Growth and What You Can Expect to Earn

With job growth of 12 percent for middle school teachers, 6 percent for high school teachers, and 11 to 19 percent for postsecondary educators, the forecast for future teachers of all subjects is looking bright through 2024. And for those who wish to teach science, there is the added bonus of knowing that STEM will continue to be a priority well into the future. There is also a shortage of teaching professionals in the field. According to the National Science Teachers Association, a group that promotes the interests of people involved in science education, many schools find it challenging to attract suitable candidates to fill vacancies in the sciences. In a poll conducted by the group, nearly 60 percent of respondents said their school was hard-pressed to recruit science teachers.

Salaries for teachers vary considerably depending on the states where they teach. Other variables that will make a difference are having a graduate degree and the number of years you have been teaching. What type of school you are teaching in also has an effect. For example, private schools pay teachers significantly less than public schools because public school teachers typically belong to labor unions that negotiate salaries for their members. Moreover, teachers with master's degrees earn about $7,000 more than teachers with bachelor's degrees. Teachers with doctorate degrees earn about $14,000 more than teachers who hold bachelor's degrees. According to the Bureau of Labor Statistics, the average high school science teacher makes about $56,200 a year.

And along with the paycheck comes the satisfaction that you are helping to prepare young people for futures in which they may discover a new drug that cures a terrible disease, or help find ways for humans to travel into deep space, or invent new technology that eliminates pollution. Alfonso Gonzalez, a middle school science teacher in Chimacum, Washington, summed up why he chose the profession on the website of Concordia University in Portland, Oregon. He said, "I like teaching science because I can explore the world and even the universe with my students in fun and exciting ways! We get to question phenomena kids might take for granted and seek answers to our questions by researching and doing experiments! How can you beat that?"

Find Out More

National Association of Biology Teachers (NABT)
PO Box 3363
Warrenton, VA 20188
fax: (202) 962-3939
website: www.nabt.org

This professional association for biology teachers provides publications and similar resources to help biology teachers lead their classes. The group also assists teachers in setting up and acting as advisers to NABT Bio Clubs, in which student members pursue experiments and projects related to learning about biology.

National Earth Science Teachers Association (NESTA)
PO Box 271654
Fort Collins, CO 80527
phone: (201) 519-1071
website: www.nestanet.org

NESTA promotes excellence in earth and space science. NESTA holds conferences, posts job openings, and offers resources for educators and print publications such as the quarterly journal the *Earth Scientist*.

National Science Teachers Association (NSTA)
1840 Wilson Blvd.
Arlington, VA 22201
phone: (703) 243-7100
website: www.nsta.org

The NSTA promotes excellence and innovation in science teaching. The organization has fifty-five thousand members comprising science teachers, science supervisors, administrators, scientists, and business and industry representatives. Its website offers resources for science teachers, professional publications, and articles on classroom safety, climate change, and other subjects.

Teach for America
25 Broadway, Floor 12
New York, NY 10004
website: www.teachforamerica.org

Teach for America is a twenty-five-year-old organization that recruits, trains, and supports college graduates it places in schools in urban and rural communities affected by poverty. Visitors to its website can learn how to apply to the program and read stories about people who have participated.

Veterinarian

A Few Facts

Number of Jobs

As of 2014, about 78,300

Salaries

As of 2014, the average salary is $87,590.

Educational Requirements

Doctorate in veterinary medicine

Personal Qualities

Love of animals, compassion, problem-solving skills, good communicator

Work Setting

Varies from small animal clinics to farms, ranches, universities, and research centers

Future Job Outlook

Job growth of 9 percent through 2024, which is faster than average

More than Cats and Dogs

When most people think of a veterinarian they picture a white-coated man or woman who runs a small neighborhood animal clinic or hospital and whose patients are mostly pet cats and dogs. This is an accurate picture because 60 percent of all people who graduate from vet school do operate such practices. But that leaves another 40 percent of the profession that most people know little about, making the field a lot broader than you might think. In fact, veterinarians may be taking care of large animals like horses, or exotic animals that might be found in zoos, circuses, or theme parks.

But even that seems pretty familiar when compared to what Jessie Sanders does. Sanders, who lives in Santa Cruz, California, is an aquatic veterinarian. She runs a mobile practice and her patients are fish such as those found in backyard ponds or in large aquariums. In an interview with the magazine *KOI USA*—a magazine serving readers who raise colorful koi fish in backyard ponds—Sanders describs her job:

There is a new figure on the horizon . . . your local fish veterinarian. Yes, fish veterinarian: a veterinarian that treats the critters that live underwater instead of those on land. You may envision now your local cat [or] dog veterinarian donning a wetsuit and jumping in your pond with stethoscope at the ready, but this usually isn't the case. We like to stay dry as much as possible, which usually means we only get half soaking wet at the worst. I am a fish veterinarian (or aquatic veterinarian if you prefer). I am capable of giving your fish all the health assistance I can, just like your local small animal veterinarian would do for your cat or dog. We are a new breed of veterinarians that are slowly starting to spread.

Most people would also be surprised to know that veterinarians also play a critical role in the health of the world's human population in the fields of food safety and production as well as disease prevention and treatment. For instance, research performed by veterinarians has helped cure, treat, or prevent about a dozen diseases in humans, according to the American Academy of Neurology. A few examples are malaria, mumps, and rubella. Veterinarians have also eliminated more than a dozen diseases in chickens and steers, making the food supply safer.

Traits of a Veterinarian

If you want to be a vet, you've got to love animals. That's a given. But that's not the only personality trait that matters if you want to work with animals. Working with patients who can't use words to explain where it hurts or what is wrong with them poses some unique challenges. "Doctors can talk to their patients . . . and always have access to other humans they can talk to about their patients," says Melissa Kaplan in an essay on the animal care website anapsid.org. "Veterinarians' patients, on the other hand, can't tell the vet what is wrong, what hurts, whether they are nauseous, have trouble seeing [or] that there is something stuck deep

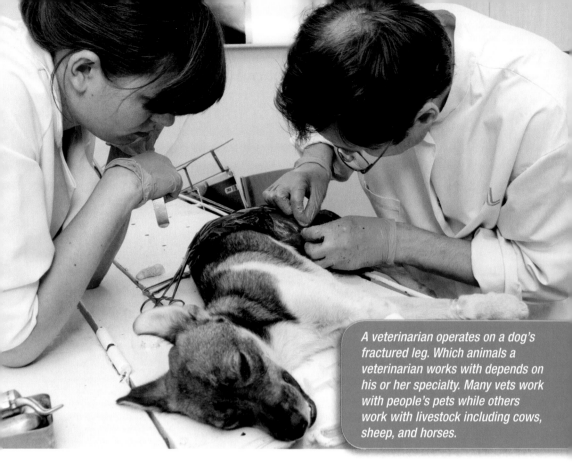

A veterinarian operates on a dog's fractured leg. Which animals a veterinarian works with depends on his or her specialty. Many vets work with people's pets while others work with livestock including cows, sheep, and horses.

inside their ear." Moreover, unlike (most) human doctors, veterinarians risk being bitten, kicked, or scratched by patients who are fearful, anxious, and in pain. Having a lot of empathy and being able to read an animal's body language for signs of stress will help the vet quickly put an animal at ease, lessening the chance for injury.

A good understanding of animal behavior is not the only trait vets need, however. Veterinarians also need people skills because they often deal with pet owners who are anxious about the health of their much-beloved animals. Business skills are also essential, particularly for those who establish their own veterinary practices, because they will need to keep appointments straight and maintain sufficient medicines and supplies on hand. They will also hire and manage employees to assist them, such as veterinary technicians, receptionists, and clerical staff members—another reason people skills are vital for veterinarians.

Getting into Veterinary School

Becoming a veterinarian takes a minimum of eight years of education after high school, including four years to receive an undergraduate degree and at least another four years to complete vet school. And as with physicians, veterinarians can go on to specialize in specific areas of veterinary medicine.

Among the veterinary specialties are cardiology, internal medicine, neurology, oncology, and surgery. Becoming a specialist in those fields may require three to five years of extra training. Pet owners are typically referred to specialists when their animals' primary veterinarians need backup. For example, a neurologist might assist when an animal is having trouble walking, is shaking, or shows troubling changes in behavior. Since animals get cancer, too, an oncologist may be needed to provide radiation or chemotherapy drugs to treat tumors. And if surgery is needed for whatever reason, the more complicated cases may be referred to a veterinary surgeon. Other choices for prospective veterinary specialists are equine medicine and surgery (which focuses on the care of horses), food, animal medicine and surgery, and anesthesiology (anesthetizing animals before surgery).

Because there are far fewer veterinary schools than medical schools, it is much more difficult to win admission to vet school

Always on Call

"Probably the biggest challenge for me as a solo practitioner in a small, rural town with a mixed practice, is if I'm not here, we're not open. That means I'm on call every day of the week, unless I'm out of town. The hard part is carving out time for yourself and your family. . . . I grumble, gripe, curse and mumble around when the phone rings at night but I like it, it's fulfilling. If I could go back in time I'd still become a vet."

Terry Lohmann, quoted in *High Plains Journal*, "The Secret Life of a Veterinarian," February 15, 2016. www.hpj.com.

than medical school. Half of all applicants are rejected by the thirty schools that offer such programs. This sobering fact means that the successful candidate must be an excellent science student who does well on graduate school entrance examinations and has completed all the prerequisite courses required by the school.

In addition, students need to demonstrate that they have already volunteered or worked in the field. So if you think you would like to be a vet one day it makes sense to begin getting that experience as early as high school or certainly by the start of college. You can accomplish that by shadowing a local veterinarian, volunteering or working at an animal clinic, or participating in an extracurricular program focusing on animal care.

Challenging Curriculum

Once enrolled in vet school a period of intense study begins, and even high-achieving students can be in for a shock. When Joyce Wick was interviewed by the *High Plains Journal* in 2016, a weekly newspaper in Dodge City, Kansas, she was in her first year at Kansas State University Veterinary School. Grateful to have gotten in, Wick was still getting used to the difficult curriculum. "School has been really challenging for me. You sit down and study the material, but the results are much harder to get. I am very content with B's at this moment," she said.

Students spend their veterinary school years participating in a combination of classroom lectures, laboratory studies, and clinical rotations. In class they'll study animal anatomy, disease prevention, and treatment. Later on, they'll have hands-on experience in veterinary hospitals where they'll have the opportunities to discover which specialties they may consider pursuing.

Working Conditions

As with physicians, many vets work overtime, nights, and weekends and are on call for emergencies. There are also hazards of the trade: A large animal such as a horse might kick the veterinarian

Being Prepared for Anything

"I'm getting to that age where people ask me am I considering retirement. But I love my job, I'm still excited by my job. . . . It's a challenge. My patient cannot tell me what's wrong. I never know what's gonna walk through the door. It may be shots, been hit by a car, fighting disease. I love it."

James Creek, quoted in *Fort Bend Star*, "Sugar Land Veterinarian Helps Pets," February 24, 2016. www.fortbendstar.com.

trying to treat it. A frightened dog can bite or a cat might scratch, wounding the veterinarian. (Sanders, the aquatic veterinarian, was once knocked down by current from an electric eel, after the tip of her finger accidentally came into contact with the fish.) In addition, tough decisions have to be made, such as whether to end the life of an animal that is suffering with no chance of getting better. Euthanizing a pet—sometimes referred to as putting an animal down or to sleep—may be the right decision but can also be tough on the veterinarian administering the fatal dose of medication that stops the pet's heart.

In an essay written for the website Conscious Cat, veterinarian Elizabeth Colleran of Chico, California, said euthanizing a pet is the most difficult part of her job.

> While in many respects, I think of euthanasia as a privilege to perform when suffering is the alternative, nevertheless, it is always hard on me. Not as hard as it is for clients who don't want to give up, but emotionally trying. I watched my Dad suffer to death for three months in a [hospital] so I know how important it is to assist in ending suffering. We veterinarians think of ourselves as healers, capable of diagnosing, curing or managing illness and injury. When we can no longer do so, our role in the pet's and family's life changes. We are not allies in the fight any longer. We must advise the course to prevent suffering; sometimes that means death.

Where the Jobs Are and What They'll Pay

A career in veterinary science can be highly satisfying, making a huge difference for animals and their owners as well as for human health and the food industry. Yet it takes truly dedicated individuals to embrace such a future knowing that they would likely earn less than physicians. This is particularly important because most young vets graduate with $135,000 in debt, accounting for the money they owe for loans they took out to pay for tuition and living expenses during their four years of advanced schooling.

The good news is that veterinarians usually have few problems finding work. Their services are in greatest demand in rural parts of the country where veterinarians are needed by farmers and ranch owners who maintain herds of livestock. Veterinarians are also needed by zoos and theme parks, which often maintain large animals used in theatrical productions. In 2014, veterinarians were making an average of $87,590 a year, according to the Bureau of Labor Statistics.

The field is expected to grow by 9 percent, which is above average, adding about seven thousand jobs by 2024. That's good news for anyone who loves animals, loves science, is a strong student, and is driven to spend time working with animals in some capacity before applying to veterinary medicine college.

Find Out More

American Association of Veterinary State Boards (AAVSB)
380 W. Twenty-Second St., Suite 101
Kansas City, MO 64108
phone: (816) 931-1504
website: www.aavsb.org

The AAVSB licenses veterinarians, providing standards vets must meet in order to maintain their practices. Visitors to the group's website can find information on the educational requirements for veterinarians.

American College of Veterinary Surgeons

19785 Crystal Rock Dr., Suite 305
Germantown, MD 20874
phone: (877) 217-2287
website: www.acvs.org

The American College of Veterinary Surgeons sets surgical standards for the profession, promotes advancements in veterinary surgery, and provides surgical education programs. More than 1,853 surgeons have been credentialed through the organization. Its website has information about what surgeons do and questions to ask veterinarians.

American Veterinary Medical Association

1931 N. Meacham Rd., Suite 100
Schaumburg, IL 60173
phone: (800) 248-2862
website: www.avma.org

The American Veterinary Medical Association represents more than eighty-eight thousand veterinarians working in private and corporate practice, government, industry, academia, and uniformed services. It produces a professional journal, and its website has information on different species of animals and hot topics in veterinary medicine.

National Board of Veterinary Medical Examiners

PO Box 1356
Bismarck, ND 58502
phone: (701) 224-0332
website: www.nbvme.org

Established in 1948, the National Board of Veterinary Medical Examiners administers the computer-based North American Veterinary Licensing Examination veterinarians must take to be certified. Its website offers information about the licensing exam, self-assessments, and a discussion forum.

Judy Morgan is a veterinarian in Clayton, New Jersey. A veterinarian for more than thirty-two years, she operates two veterinary practices. Morgan is a certified veterinary acupuncturist, veterinary chiropractor, and veterinary food therapist and the author of several books on nutrition and health care for dogs.

Q: Why did you become a veterinarian?

A: When I was thirteen I had a show pony that became so lame he could no longer be ridden. We retired him to the pasture, but he could hardly walk. My riding instructor's daughter was an equine veterinarian and she came to spend the summer at the farm. She offered to perform a surgery to remove the nerves from the pony's front feet so he could walk better. She let me assist with the surgery, done right there at the farm. She instructed me in his aftercare and bandage changes. I loved everything about the process. She became my idol and I followed her everywhere. I knew then that I was going to become a veterinarian.

Q: Can you describe your typical workday?

A: I start my day around 7 a.m., working on writing and keeping up with my social media and website. I arrive at the office around 8:30, go through messages and lab work from the day before; then I see outpatient appointments until noon or 1. Then I move to surgery and inpatient care for the afternoon. Around 3 or 4 p.m. I head back to outpatient appointments until 6 or 7 p.m., depending on the day. After that, I finish phone calls that I didn't have time to get to during the day. I arrive home around 7:30 p.m.

Q: What do you like most and what do you like least about your work?

A: I enjoy surgery the most. I also enjoy working with senior pets and their owners, trying to find the best quality of life for them in their senior years. But my favorite part of my job right now is writing and public speaking. Not many veterinarians have a desire to be a public figure, but I love it. What I like least are pet owners who treat their animals like they have no feelings; owners who do the bare minimum that is legally required. I also don't like that sometimes decisions are made due to financial constraints. I don't blame the pet owners, but it is a reality we have to deal with. In a perfect world, we'd be able to treat every animal with the latest therapies, but that isn't always possible.

Q: What personal qualities do you find most valuable for being a vet?

A: Being able to talk to people, being compassionate. Most people think being a vet is all about playing with animals all day, but it's really about dealing with people. Compassion for the animals and their owners is really important. We can't be judgmental; we have to accept that not every owner deals with their pets the way we would and that not everyone has the financial resources to give the go-ahead in every situation.

Q: What advice do you have for students who might be interested in this career?

A: Take some business courses along with the math and science. Knowing how to run a business will make you much more successful. Be open to continued learning for the rest of your life. The medical field changes daily and there is always something new to learn. Definitely spend some time shadowing a veterinarian. We have had many students come spend a day or two, especially in surgery, who have left saying this is not what they want to do. Some students have decided they liked the job of the veterinary technician more than the veterinarian and have switched paths. We have even had some who decided they'd rather be the receptionist, which does not require eight years of college.

Q: Is there anything you wish you had known before choosing this career?

A: More information about business. I learned in the school of hard knocks how to run the business side of my practice. It wasn't pretty. The veterinary field has changed a lot since I graduated over thirty years ago. There is more competition and more practices are becoming corporate-owned. For some people, being an employee and working in a corporation might be the perfect match. For me, being an independent owner was the better fit. The hours can be really long, especially if you want to own your own practice. Many practices are now open seven days a week, so you need to prepare yourself to have a nontraditional schedule instead of 9–5, Monday thru Friday.

Q: Did you ever think about doing something else?

A: Not really. When I went to college, the odds of getting into vet school were 13 to 1 and there were only about 25 percent women in the field. I considered applying to medical school if I didn't get into vet school, but the sight of human blood makes me faint.

OTHER CAREERS IF YOU LIKE SCIENCE

Aquaculture Manager
Astronomer
Biologist
Chemist
Chiropractor
Coroner
Cytologist
Dental Hygienist
Dentist
Earth Scientist
Emergency Medical Technician
Food Scientist
Geneticist
Hydrologist
Immunologist
Lab Technician

Marine Biologist
Medical Technologist
Metallurgist
Meteorologist
Nurse
Oceanographer
Paleontologist
Park Ranger
Pharmacist
Physician
Physicist
Research Scientist
Seismologist
Soil Scientist
Veterinary Technician
X-ray Technician

Editor's note: The online *Occupational Outlook Handbook* of the US Department of Labor's Bureau of Labor Statistics is an excellent source of information on jobs in hundreds of career fields, including many of those listed here. The *Occupational Outlook Handbook* may be accessed online at www.bls.gov/ooh.